Asking Questions about

Asking Questions About What's on Television

Jamie Weil

Published in the United States of America by Cherry Lake Publishing
Ann Arbor, Michigan
www.cherrylakepublishing.com

Consultant: Barb Palser, Digital Media Executive; Marla Conn, ReadAbility, Inc.
Editorial direction and book production: Red Line Editorial
Book design: Sleeping Bear Press

Photo Credits: Dmitriy Karelin/Shutterstock Images, cover, 1; Pavel L./Shutterstock Images, 5, 11; Samuel H. Gottscho/Library of Congress, 6; Shutterstock Images, 8, 15, 26; Denys Prykhodov/Shutterstock Images, 12; iStockphoto, 17; Daria Zu/iStockphoto, 18; NBC/Photofest, 21; Ed Stock/iStockphoto, 22; Anatoly Tiplyashin/Shutterstock Images, 25; S. Bukley/Shutterstock Images, 28

Copyright © 2016 by Cherry Lake Publishing
All rights reserved. No part of this book may be reproduced or utilized in any form or by any means without written permission from the publisher.

Library of Congress Cataloging-in-Publication Data

Weil, Jamie.
  Asking questions about what's on television / by Jamie Weil.
    pages cm. -- (Asking questions about media)
  Includes bibliographical references and index.
    ISBN 978-1-63362-493-1 (hardcover : alk. paper) -- ISBN 978-1-63362-509-9 (pbk. : alk. paper) -- ISBN 978-1-63362-525-9 (pdf ebook) -- ISBN 978-1-63362-541-9 (hosted ebook)
  1. Television broadcasting--Juvenile literature. I. Title.

PN1992.57.W46 2015
791.45--dc23

2015005527

Cherry Lake Publishing would like to acknowledge the work of the Partnership for 21st Century Skills. Please visit www.p21.org for more information.

Printed in the United States of America
Corporate Graphics Inc.

ABOUT THE AUTHOR

Jamie Weil loves to watch TV, but she also loves to dance, swim, and hang out with real people. She lives in a small, rural town in Northern California with her family, where her favorite thing to do is to write books for young people.

TABLE OF CONTENTS

CHAPTER 1
Behind the Screen 4

CHAPTER 2
Pay for Play 10

CHAPTER 3
Tricks of the Trade 14

CHAPTER 4
Same Message, Different Response 20

CHAPTER 5
Uncovering Bias 24

THINK ABOUT IT 30
LEARN MORE 31
GLOSSARY 32
INDEX 32

Behind the Screen

The process of producing a television program looks very different from the end result you see on your screen. Your favorite half-hour show takes many hours to make. TV professionals want to entertain viewers. They use lighting, music, acting, special effects, and other **techniques** to accomplish this goal. When you see the New York City skyline on TV, you actually might be looking at a digital image. When actors jump out of airplanes on TV, they're probably standing in front of a big green screen waving their hands. Almost like magic, the whole scene comes to life through a combination of many amazing media tools. By the time your show is done, it seems perfectly natural and entertaining.

This technology magic is not the only thing happening behind the scenes of your favorite TV shows. Every TV show also sends messages, both obvious and **subtle**. You may not give much thought to the

There's a lot more going on behind the scenes of a TV show than meets the eye.

Technology has come a long way since television was invented in 1929.

messages your program is sending. However, it's important that you do.

Since its invention in 1929, the TV business has become increasingly **sophisticated**. Most programs you see on TV are not just aired to entertain viewers. They also are designed to make money or influence their audience. It's important to examine whether the show is trying to sell you or tell you something below the surface.

Why is that important? If a show is trying to sell you or tell you something, you need to know what that is so

Case Study
Television Tools

Television uses a complex, creative language made up of design, production choices, sound, lighting, and many other elements. Actors can repeat the same words and produce completely different meanings based on these elements. How these elements are organized influences what message is sent to the audience. For example, a script may call for an actor to say, "I can't find it!" If the actor is crying when he speaks this line, the viewer gets one message. If sad music, tears, and low lighting are added to the scene, the message becomes more intense. These elements may work to make the viewer feel sad, too. However, if the actor says the same line of "I can't find it!" with a goofy look on his face, the message changes. Add a silly music track and laughter in the background and the viewer is likely to laugh too.

you can make good choices and form your own opinions. It's important to be able to find both obvious and hidden messages in what you're watching.

Once you know how to recognize messages, you will learn how to analyze them. This means to pull apart the

Production elements help craft many of the messages that you see on TV.

messages and see how they are created. Then you will be able to ask the right questions to discover whether you agree with them. A big part of figuring out TV messages is having an understanding of what is important to ask.

- Who pays for the messages in TV shows and why?
- What TV tricks grab your attention?
- How do TV messages affect people differently?
- How can you uncover the points of view of those who created the TV message?

Read on to explore the answers to these questions. Learn about what goes on behind the scenes and beyond the TV screen!

Pay for Play

Messages on television are delivered in many forms. As a viewer, you receive them through commercials, news programs, movies, scripted shows, and more. The variety of screens on which viewers can watch TV is constantly increasing. Today TV can be watched on phones, tablets, car displays, and home screens of various sizes. This means TV shows are more accessible to viewers every day.

Who are the people behind these shows? Many people influence TV messages. These include writers, actors, producers, directors, and studio owners. Each group influences the messages according to its own values. When you watch a program, pay close attention to what the messages you are exposed to are trying to

The actors you see on screen are only one part of a team of TV professionals who influence what goes into a show.

If you can recognize the brands being used on a TV show, it might not be a coincidence.

sell you or tell you. Ask yourself if these values line up with your own beliefs.

One way to unravel media messages is to learn who is paying to send the message. For example, if you're watching a show on the Disney Channel, you're likely to see some commercials advertising Disney products. But Disney isn't just paying for the messages sent during commercial breaks. An actor in the show may wear a Mickey Mouse shirt or drink from a *Frozen* cup. These items are products made and sold by Disney. Disney chooses to show these things in the program in order to create interest in them. This is called product placement. It has the same purpose as a commercial but is different because it is more subtle. You have to look closely to find the message.

Product Placement

According to one study, 90 percent of households with a digital video recorder (DVR) use it to skip commercials when watching recorded programs. As viewers find more ways to skip commercials, advertisers look for more ways to sell their products within the television show itself. Companies pay big money to showcase their products in TV shows. To spot products placed in shows you watch, ask yourself these questions. What brand of phones or computers are being used? What are the characters eating? Are the characters using a particular game or toy? What are the characters wearing? If the brand name of any of these items is obvious, it might be the result of product placement.

Tricks of the Trade

Since its invention, television technology has continued to advance. TV creators invest a lot of money in technology. One reason they do this is to find the best ways to send their messages while also entertaining their audience. Special effects can grab a viewer's attention. What technology tricks do TV creators use to get your attention?

One tool TV creators use is the green screen. A green screen is just what it sounds like: a plain, green screen. It is used as a background for certain scenes, but it is

The green screen makes it possible for another background to be added to a shot.

not the final background the TV audience sees. For example, say an actress is acting out a scene of a woman hanging from the edge of a cliff about to fall. The actress stands in front of a green screen with her hands reaching up. After the scene is filmed, editors use digital technology to insert an image of a cliff where the green screen was to make that actress appear to be hanging from a cliff.

Another special technology technique used in TV involves sound. Different sounds affect your brain in

THE GREEN SCREEN

The green screen is a technology that helps studios create image effects. Actors stand in front of it to act out a scene, and the screen is later replaced with a digital image of something else. Why is the screen green? Because green doesn't interfere with the actors' skin tones. After filming, a specialist uses a process called chroma keying on the computer to recreate the scene. Chroma keying removes a particular color (*chroma* is the Greek word for color) from video and inserts (or keys) another color. When done well, it's difficult for the viewer to **distinguish** between a green screen and a real background.

different ways. Sound editors play with this **dynamic** to create different emotional reactions in their audience. For example, in comedy shows laughter can be used to emphasize certain jokes. When you watch a comedy show and hear what sounds like an audience of people laughing at the show's scenes, the show may seem funnier to you. Often, laugh tracks have been used to create this effect. Laugh tracks are prerecorded sounds of an audience laughing. They can be added to the show

Do you enjoy a show more if you hear an audience laughing and applauding?

[ASKING QUESTIONS ABOUT MEDIA]

by editors. However, some shows are filmed in front of a live audience. In the past, some studios hired professional laughers to sit in the audience while these show were being filmed. Today, the popularity of laugh tracks and live audience laughter has declined. But some modern shows, such as *The Big Bang Theory*, still film

Sound is an important element in TV programming.

before live audiences. While watching your favorite comedies, take notice if you hear laughing in the background. If you do, does it make the show seem funnier to you?

Images and sounds aren't the only unnatural effects used in TV programs. Editing is another technique to create certain effects that might not appear naturally. Reality TV is filled with such examples. In those shows, the producers film many hours of content. Then editors **filter** out the elements they don't want to include in the half-hour or hour that makes it on the air. For example, producers of the show *Survivor* might want to emphasize conflict between two contestants in an episode. So for that episode, editors will use footage that shows the contestants arguing, while cutting out scenes that show them getting along.

CHAPTER 4

Same Message, Different Response

Television creators adjust their messages to reach different audiences because they know people respond to messages differently. One way they do this is through emotional appeals that attempt to connect with different viewers.

For example, the creators of the weight-loss reality show *The Biggest Loser* try to send the message that managing your health—and specifically your weight—is important. They know that their viewers don't all respond the same way to their techniques. So they use many different methods to grab viewers' attention.

The show creators know that some viewers are likely inspired by watching the contestants working hard in the gym, so part of the show centers on workouts. Other viewers might relate to the contestants' personal stories. To grab these viewers' attention, the producers include emotional interviews of the contestants talking about their weight-loss journeys. The show creators also know

Reality shows such as The Biggest Loser *find different ways to reach different viewers.*

American Idol is one of the most successful reality TV shows of all time.

that another set of viewers may get fired up by competition, so each week the show features some type of physical contest between each trainer's teams. Then the teams go head-to-head in a weigh-in that results in one contestant being sent home. To reach viewers who struggle with their diet, *The Biggest Loser* creators include tips on cooking healthy food. Contestants also meet with doctors to show the audience how their health has improved since they've been on the show. All of these techniques send the same message—that being healthy is important—but each method is designed to reach a specific audience.

Although it is a reality show, it's important to remember that *The Biggest Loser* is entertainment. Even reality-based shows are somewhat staged in order to emphasize the message the show's creators want to send. And the producers use creative language to make the show emotional and dramatic, just as TV creators do on scripted shows you watch.

Reality TV

Reality-based shows give the viewers a sense of watching unscripted, real-life situations play out on their televisions. The public's introduction to reality TV came in 1948 with Allen Funt's hidden-camera show **Candid** *Camera*. In 2000, CBS launched the modern wave of reality TV with its hit competitive survival show *Survivor*. Today, the range of reality TV is vast, from dating shows such as *The Bachelor* to singing contests such as *The Voice* and *American Idol*.

CHAPTER 5

Uncovering Bias

People who create television shows have their own opinions and points of view, just as you do. Their views can influence the message they are sending viewers. How can you uncover TV producers' points of view? Start by examining how the show's message makes you feel. Are you uncomfortable? If so, your values and beliefs may be different from those who created the message. Does the message make you happy? Then your values likely align with those who created it.

When you analyze point of view by using your feelings as your guide, you can spot propaganda more easily. Propaganda is the use of biased claims to sell an idea or product. Looking closely at what a TV show's message includes and excludes can help you identify what it's trying to sell you or tell you.

For example, consider the concept of family. Different shows tell you what families look like. TV shows

The setting of a TV show can send a message about how "average" families live.

[ASKING QUESTIONS ABOUT MEDIA]

The varied cast of Modern Family *portrays different ways that families can be composed.*

indirectly send the message that average families are made up of a certain arrangement and look a certain way. According to many shows, average families have a mom and a dad, children, and a pet. Obviously, not all families look like this.

Some points of view can be tricky to uncover. Sometimes programs feature characters that the audience is supposed to relate to, but does not. This can happen when those characters act in a questionable manner. For example, in Marvel's *Agent Carter*, the title character goes behind the back of her boss to clear the name of a friend. Some viewers may relate to the title character's action. But some viewers might find going behind someone's back wrong. So what is the purpose of the situation? It might be to give the message that in life, sometimes the line between right and wrong is blurred.

Some programs share points of view centered on issues or topics that some people consider **taboo** to discuss in modern culture. For example, the hit show

Family Diversity

Many American TV programs such as *Modern Family* show that family combinations can take many forms. *The Cosby Show* revolved around an upper-class African-American family in New York City in the 1980s. *Black-ish* showed the lives of an upper-class African-American family in California when it debuted in 2014. *Fresh Off the Boat* is a 2015 sitcom that featured Asian-American immigrants. These shows offer different points of view through the way the characters handle a variety of situations the different types of families find themselves in.

Pretty Little Liars deals with teen pregnancy, bullying, eating disorders, and other problems usually not shown on entertainment TV.

Television is a big part of the lives of many young Americans. As you watch TV, keep in mind the messages your favorite shows send. From the surface level to behind the scenes, there's a lot more going on than you might realize.

The cast of *The Big Bang Theory* has won multiple awards.

Case Study
Stereotypes on TV

Stereotypes are descriptions that give a general, and sometimes false, impression of a person using broad details. Some TV shows use stereotypes as shortcuts to character development. If a character on a show fits into a stereotype, viewers are automatically familiar with that character without needing to know much about their specific backstory. For example, on the sitcom *The Big Bang Theory*, the character Penny fits into the "dumb blonde" stereotype. Her friends fit the "genius nerd" stereotype. When the characters interact, the viewer knows what to expect because they've seen similar characters on other shows. However, some of the most popular characters on TV play against stereotypes, meaning the characters are not what viewers would expect. One example is the character Abby on the investigation show *NCIS*. She is known for her gothic fashion style, jet-black hair, red lipstick, and multiple tattoos. Viewers might expect Abby to be **rebellious** and anti-authority. But she is also a brilliant forensic scientist and computer expert.

THINK ABOUT IT

When you watch a TV show, can you tell what it's trying to sell you or tell you while it entertains you?

Think about who pays for the messages in a TV show—what do they have to gain by your viewership?

What tricks of the trade do the programs that you watch use to get your attention?

What different TV techniques are used to reach different audiences in the shows you watch?

Can you tell the point of view of a show and whether its message matches your own values?

LEARN MORE

FURTHER READING

Kelly, Shannon. *Reality TV*. Detroit, MI: Lucent Books, 2013.

Mussari, Mark. *American Life and Television: From I Love Lucy to Mad Men*. New York: Marshall Cavendish, 2013.

Spilsbury, Richard and Louise Spilsbury. *The Television*. Chicago: Heinemann Library, 2012.

WEB LINKS

Early Television Foundation and Museum
www.earlytelevision.org/
Learn more about the history of the early days of television.

PBS Kids Go!: Don't Buy It—Get Media Smart!
www.pbskids.org/dontbuyit/entertainment/tvvslife_1.html
Activities that help young people develop critical thinking skills about the media.

The Center for Media Literacy
www.medialit.org
An educational organization that provides leadership, public education, professional development, and educational resources.

[ASKING QUESTIONS ABOUT MEDIA]

GLOSSARY

candid (KAN-did) when people act naturally instead of posed, as in picture and film

distinguish (diss-TING-gwish) to set one thing apart from other things because of a particular quality

dynamic (dye-NAM-ik) the way that people behave with each other because of a particular situation

filter (FIL-tur) to hold back elements or modify something in some way

rebellious (ri-BEL-yuhss) likely to fight against the people in charge of something

sophisticated (suh-FISS-tuh-kay-tid) developed and complex

subtle (SUHT-uhl) difficult to notice or see

taboo (ta-BOO) a subject that may upset or offend people

techniques (tek-NEEKS) methods or ways of doing something that require skill

INDEX

Agent Carter, 26–27
American Idol, 23

Bachelor, The, 23
Big Bang Theory, The, 18, 29
Biggest Loser, The, 20–23
Black-ish, 27

Candid Camera, 23
Cosby Show, The, 27

Disney Channel, 12–13

Fresh Off the Boat, 27

green screen, 4, 14–15, 16

laughter, 7, 16, 18–19

Modern Family, 27

NCIS, 29

Pretty Little Liars, 28
product placement, 12–13

Survivor, 19, 23

Voice, The, 23